I Notice

A Step-by-Step Guide to Transform
Student Potential Through Building
Intentional Relationships

Claire E. Hallinan

ISBN: 978-1-7330356-1-3

Contact Claire E. Hallinan:

claire.e.hallinan@gmail.com

https://claireehallinan.wordpress.com/

Dedication

To Ms. Takahashi

We can never obtain peace in the outer world until we make peace with ourselves.

~Dalai Lama

Table of Contents

Introduction

Many years ago, one passionate young principal announced at the beginning of a random staff meeting, "Relationships, relationships, relationships." The teachers looked at each other. *Haven't we already established relationships with our students? Why do we have to make more of an effort? What does he want us to do?* We wondered if we were missing something. If you are a teacher, a coach, and/or a parent, relationships are very important. But how do you know if you have a good relationship with each individual student? Why does a relationship come before actual "learning"?

While we can't confirm the strength of our relationship with our students, let's think about the word "relate." When you see your friend picking up their water bottle, opening the lid, lifting the bottle, and bringing it to their mouth, you unknowingly reach for your own water bottle. This happens because mirror neurons are firing in your brain. Mirror neurons are a type of brain cell that is wired to respond both when you perform an action and when you witness someone else performing the same action. Our brains are made to relate to one another.

Similarly, when the main character in a movie discovers that they have a terminal illness, you feel sad—you may even cry. When you join a group of friends who are laughing about a joke, you start smiling, even though you may not know what the joke is about. When you "read" other people's minds and feel empathy for them, the same part of your brain (mirror neurons) is firing and re-wiring.

As you can see, our brains are social organs that respond to one another. That means we were born to be social creatures. However, you might feel strong connections with certain people, but not with others. One of the reasons that this occurs is due to "intention." When you want to relate to someone, you make an effort. You might say "hi" or smile. Perhaps you might want to talk about a similar interest that you share with that person. In the adult world, you have the freedom to pick and choose who you hang out with.

If you are working with youth, adult-world rules don't apply. Every child is important and unique. Every child needs an intentional connection with you in order for them to succeed. They should feel safe and trust in you so that they will want to hear what you teach each day. You know all about this and you relate with youth so well—that's why you work with youth.

Also, it's true that the time you spend with youth is not necessarily always pleasurable. Some days are rather chaotic. Do mirror neurons translate these difficult and negative emotions? Probably. That is why if we are frustrated when we are giving good advice, our students will pick up on our frustration rather than what we are telling them. As this frustrating cycle continues, the wall between us and our students becomes taller. How can we deliver the best advice in our best condition so that our students are willing to listen to us? I finally discovered that everything starts from within ourselves.

I am writing this book to help your students learn how to perform their best in the field they share with you. To accomplish this task, you will learn how to shift your thinking patterns, how to connect to students and to yourself, and what message it is that you want to deliver. Here, I share my own experiences with you, mostly from my career as an elementary school teacher. But I also include experiences from my work as a pre-school gymnastics coach and as a private piano instructor. So even if you are not a school teacher, you will learn how to maximize your target learner's performance by reading the following chapters. Just substitute your role with "teacher" and your target learners with "students."

Are you ready to fire your neurons? Here we go!

Chapter 1

—

Positive Impact through Intentional Relationships

Educators' Dilemma

Teachers get frustrated when students don't perform as they expect them to. When this happens, teachers—especially good ones—reflect on the situation. "Hmmm, I wonder why it didn't work?" Then, teachers research and reteach the same concept with more effective strategies. And yet, there are some students who still don't get it. What happens next? Teachers get frustrated. Again. Who has been trapped in this vicious cycle before? This instructional cycle is a typical, commonly used protocol in teaching and learning that all teachers should follow. But do teachers need to get frustrated every time students don't accomplish as much as they hope they will?

We often experience frustrating moments on a daily basis because we are always focusing on our children's achievements. We chose to be educators because we love kids and/or teaching certain skills to youths. And we want all learners to be successful in the area they are in, but we might question ourselves. Why do things go smoothly on some occasions but not others, even though we always intend to create positive outcomes for our kids?

We also notice that certain people respond to instruction quite well while others don't. Even when we use the same approach, performance levels vary among students. To solve this problem "differentiation" became a trend in the current education fields. Kids learn in different styles, at different paces, and at different levels. In the National Board for Professional Teaching Standards, differentiation in instruction is one of the four major components that all applicants are required to participate in.

One of the most commonly used differentiated instructional models in the current classroom setting is ability grouping. With ability grouping, teachers divide the students into small groups and provide them with the appropriate level of academic instructions and activities. How is this form of differentiated instruction effective?

According to Australian Professor John Hattie's study "Visible Learning for Teachers," the student's achievement is influenced by several factors that are categorized through six different people: students, teachers, family, school, peers, and principals. Under each person, several approaches were performed. Hattie's team studied them to determine which strategies were most effective on the student's achievement. Hattie then ranked the educational approaches by the effect size, with the median at a little over 0.4.

Ability grouping scored .18, which was not so bad. But it's not too good either.

What exact learning factor makes a difference in children's perception and, consequently, their performance? Is there something else beyond the instructional factors?

Hattie's study concluded that the most effective strategy was "Feedback" (1.13). The feedback process is to offer and to accept. Once a learner accepts it, he will reflect on the previous performance and plan for improvement.

This brings us back to the beginning of the circle. Feedback alone doesn't work well in most cases. For educators, this creates a dilemma. What else can we do to ensure that kids give their best performance during their time with us?

When feedback is appropriately used, teaching and learning happens actively and simultaneously. It's not just teaching but also learning. Then that magical moment of the most powerful learning experience shines through. While teachers/coaches obtain expertise and execute it in the best way that learners can master, the learners sharpen their "desire" to learn.

While feedback is a simple task, the learners' "desire" to learn can grow from the relationships they have with their teachers/coaches. The young learners' achievement depends on the **relationships between them and their teachers**.

Relationships Matter

Imagine someone in your life with whom you have a special relationship. And imagine someone with whom you don't have an enjoyable relationship. What makes the difference between them? Positive relationships cheer up your life, of course. And there are so many people in this world with whom you can connect very easily. The opposite is also true. Yes, there are so many people in this world

who are difficult to connect with. Whether it's with students in tɪ.
classroom or athletes in sports, we want to make intentional
relationships. The assumption we often create is, "I have already
established great relationships with my students. Why bother now?"
Are our learners going to say the same thing? Chances are they might.
Or they might not. Let's untangle this complexity.

When I was in seventh grade, my friend told me that she could live
all by herself, without depending on anyone. I argued, "Well, that is
impossible. You would technically live in a place by yourself, but you
would be renting a place from someone. You would have to buy food
from someone. You could live without talking to anyone, but you
would always be depending on someone else." She didn't like my idea,
but she didn't disagree with me either. This conversation reminded
me of how I was connected to so many different people, things, and
places in my life. I remember that I felt somewhat strange and happy
at the same time.

When we think about our lives, we realize that we all depend on
each other—directly and indirectly. We also impact other people's
lives. If this is true, why don't we care about each other? We are
linked to other people. That is a relationship. According to a Harvard

m 2017, having good relationships boosts people's longevity.

to imagine that having significant connections can make you peaceful, happy, and calm. When you feel content, good chemicals, such as dopamine and oxytocin, make your immune system stronger. In the meantime, your stress hormones decrease. No wonder happy people live longer! Even if you ignore the longevity benefits, why would you want to purposely avoid this happy feeling? Building a relationship is not a difficult task, yet it might be tricky in some ways.

I would like to propose three different relationship models, inspired by the states of matter: solid, gas, and liquid.

1. **Solid Relationships**: If it is a hard solid, it's unbreakable. Just like iron and wood, it has no flexibility. True, it won't break. But there is also no room to tweak it or make changes. If it's made of something else, like glass, once it slips from your hands, it breaks into small pieces. You cannot fix it. The Solid Relationship seems like a strong relationship, but, in actuality, it is either impossible to change or too fragile to sustain.

2. **Gas Relationships**: Many gasses are invisible. Colored gas is often toxic. Even if you can see the particles, they are constantly moving around. Each particle rarely gets to meet other particles. Even if one does meet another, they most likely won't see each other again. The Gas Relationship is a "don't-care" relationship. It means that you can genuinely express your passion to someone, but he/she will either ignore you or simply pretend to listen. How sad is that?

3. **Liquid Relationships**: A liquid's shape changes based on the shape of the container it's in. If one shape doesn't work, you can simply change the container to adjust it. Relationships can be flexible and fixable, especially if they are important. A liquid is always together and moves fluidly toward the same direction. This is, I suggest, the ideal type of relationship you want to form with others.

To build and maintain a Liquid Relationship, both parties must share a common goal. You and another person are both moving toward the same direction. You must listen to each other. Not one way but both ways. The student who is quiet doesn't necessarily have a good relationship with you. Some kids are afraid of speaking up.

Teachers and coaches need to create a space where kids can share their achievements, concerns, and questions. Understanding learners' perceptions is essential for educators. When learners embrace their challenges, their engagement maximizes. As you understand the depth of your learners' insight, you can adjust your teaching plan. Yes, this will mean changing the shape of the liquid relationship container. In any relationship, you will face some challenges. To keep the best kind of relationship, you have to admit your mistakes and try to find possible solutions together. This will let you continue your journey toward your common goals.

If you want to help your students achieve their goals, you'll need to make sure that you have a Liquid Relationship with them. By creating this kind of relationship, you are encouraging their success by showing that you care.

What You Will Learn

In this book, you will learn how to assess your current relationships with your learners (students/athletes), how to build the relationships better, and how to maintain them positively by using some techniques from the mindfulness and growth mindsets. With acceptance, breathing, courage, compassion, consistency, and a willingness for collaboration, you will be able to maintain this Liquid Relationship so that your learners can maximize their potential. When kids trust you in a well-established relationship, they are ready to perform at the next level.

There is no perfect recipe for building a relationship because it often takes time to trust someone. But with effective ingredients and consistency, a trustful relationship can be built. In this book, I will show you examples of how to incorporate ingredients so that you can become confident. It is essential for you to tweak the recipe and stay consistent. One day you may feel so successful, and another day you may get discouraged. If your intention is to connect, discouragement will not always remain. Unsuccessful experiences will provide you with the opportunity to look at the situation from a different perspective. Rather than stop you, these negative instances encourage you to continue working on the process.

Let's talk about the major ingredients for students' success through building relationships.

Mindfulness is the first ingredient. This will help you make connections within yourself. When you have achieved well-being, you can start cultivating relationships with others. Your well-being contributes to relationship building with compassion by ensuring that your approach toward your learners is positive—in attitude, through the decisions you make, and in the words you speak.

I have seen tremendous social and academic growth in my students since I adopted mindfulness in my teaching practices. Later, I found that students with mindfulness could understand the concept of growth mindsets in depth, and could therefore apply them easily into their own lives. Our minds are smarter than we think they are because we can grow them if we train them. Just as physical exercises make our muscles stronger, we can strengthen our brains. What we must do is to notice each present moment. Then our brains can be re-wired to adopt better thinking habits.

Research shows that daily mindfulness practice can re-wire your neuroplasticity. Instead of reacting to an event, your brain will learn to pause so that it can make better decisions. For instance, when you feel frustrated with a learner, you might raise your voice or talk fast like a machine gun. This is because a part of the brain called the amygdala is translating your anger. But a loud voice and too much talking probably won't bring good results. What if you pause and quietly say, "I will talk about this when I am calm"?

A growth mindset is another game changer in the learner's achievement (Dweck 2009). People with fixed mindsets believe their talent is fixed; when they think their talent is used up, or when they face challenges, they concede defeat. In Dweck's study, students who were encouraged to make an effort performed better than those who were praised for how smart they were when they faced the same challenges. In short, people with a growth mindset often outperform those with a fixed mindset. Why is this? People with a growth mindset believe in their talents as abilities that they can develop and build on. Successes are valued as something you achieve through practice and effort—not as gifts bestowed upon you at birth that require no effort. Michael Phelps' desire to win, and his years of dedicated practice, is a prime example of the growth mindset.

By building relationships, you will help your learners uncover their best potential. Most likely you'll discover yours too.

The practical tasks are organized into six weeks. To achieve the best result for your relationship building, I recommend cumulating k's new challenge with a previous task. It sounds like a lot, y, it should only take 5-10 minutes a day (even if you add several activities), because most of the activities are embedded into the time you spend with your students.

You are going to learn how to make kids perform at their best by building intentional relationships with them. You will support their goals and dreams not only with your guidance, but also through the intentional relationships that you will establish.

To begin this program, I want you to pull out a new journal or open a new word document on your computer. It doesn't have to be fancy, just simple and consistent. Self-reflection is the key to your success! Each journal entry will make you feel accomplished with what you do every day.

Let's work together. During our journey, you are welcome to ask me any questions by email at claire.e.hallinan@gmail.com. First, we are marching into the initial evaluation of the current relationship. This relationship will impact the learner's performance/achievement. That's what we care about.

Keep Your Journal

A daily reflection will maximize your learning. Why? Because you are incorporating what you learn into your own story. Storytelling strengthens your learning memories, making them more accessible in the future. To make journaling easy for you, I made blank worksheets which you can find in the Appendix. Feel free to copy and use them.

Also, if you want to work with a partner, invite them! I will send your friend the journal worksheets FREE! Email me at claire.e.hallinan@gmail.com. Collaboration will strengthen your learning. According to Hattie's study, peer tutoring is a highly rated effective learning strategy. When you share your experiences with a partner, you always gain knowledge.

Are you ready? Here we go!

Evaluate Current Relationships

Recently, I found out that I might unconsciously harm students with some of the phrases that I use. Even if our intentions are good, negative phrases and/or judgments not only discourage students, but might also traumatize them.

I often tell my students about two different scars. "When you fall from your bike and get an 'owie' on your knee, it hurts, but the pain soon disappears. Another scar is invisible. When you carelessly use words, the scar in that person's heart can become permanent." Although it is an invisible mark, it will not go away like a physical scar would. That's why we tell kids to think before they talk. This advice applies to adults too. Sometimes we unconsciously say things to kids. Though we don't mean to cause pain, our words might negatively affect our kids—especially if we haven't yet built a well-established relationship with them. We must remember that any harsh expressions that we use can destroy trust and respect.

Here are some questions to help you evaluate your habits. You will receive one point for each phrase you have **ever** said to anyone (both adults and children included):

1. You are lazy.

2. You are not trying hard enough.

3. You are not focused.

4. You are always making excuses.

5. You should do better.

How many points did you score? If you have ever used even one of these phrases, it is time to think seriously about your relationships with the people around you, especially children.

First, phrases that start with "You" are evaluative (judgmental) statements. Your evaluation might be accurate, however, your learner might not see things the way you see them. We want our learners' academic skills or athletic abilities to improve; our job is to make our learners believe that it is important, so they desire improvement. We cannot assume that all students have a strong mentality simply because they like school or sports. While we are teaching certain subjects or skills, we are simultaneously nurturing students' mental strengths. In most cases, these evaluative statements do not encourage children in any fields, whether school- or sports-related.

When we notice that a child is not focused, what do we want her to do? Our goal is for this child to be focused. What is the best way to make this child focus? Saying "you are not focused" won't make her focus. But it will likely create a wall between the two of you.

Regardless of whether you think you have a "good enough" relationship or "want-to-improve" relationship, we are here together. Instead of building walls that separate us from each other, we will create pipes to connect us to one another. We will explore the daily SIMPLE exercise over the next six weeks to help transform our relationships with our young learners. As our relationships improve, our learners will consequently maximize their potential to a level that we expect! Even better, these youngsters will recognize the possibility that they can perform better than their potential. Although individual practice will benefit you, working with a partner is ideal. By working this program with a partner, we will deepen our knowledge of relationships and (as a bonus) strengthen the relationship with our partner.

<Journal Entry> (See Appendix A)

Here are the first three entries to begin our journey. After you complete them, meet up with your partner and discuss what you have written.

1) List some of your learners with whom you want to improve your current relationship, 2) list why you want to improve your relationship, and 3) list what you hope this improved relationship will accomplish.

Example:

1) Josh

2) He is lazy and doesn't seem like he's listening to me. He doesn't try anything by himself, although he has so much potential!

3) I want him to pay attention when I talk or give directions.

Simple enough? Oh yeah.

Chapter 2

Observation Not Judgment

Week 1: I Notice Statement in Relationship with Children

This week, I challenge you to a somewhat awkward task. Instead of using "You" statements, try to use "I notice" statements (Fey, Funk 1995). Describe what kids are doing with as much detail as possible. If you **whisper** to someone, talk privately, or at least use a calm voice, that is a plus.

We all know that public recognition of certain negative behavior can cause a child humiliation, even if we are joking. A personalized "I notice" comment will avoid that, especially if made without any judgment. Simple examples might be, "I notice you are thinking of something else," "I notice you are about to start your task," or "I notice your legs are not straight."

In other cases, educators often publicly acknowledge their students' positive performance in the learning community. In this instance, our intention is to build our students' self-confidence and to motivate other students. But if your intention is to build a relationship with your student, make your compliment in private. Forget about other outcomes and focus on the relationship because this is your opportunity. For instance, "Mary, I notice your toes are pointy," or "I notice you are using subtraction on this problem." Yes, share random things that you notice and practice during as many occasions as you can. Just acknowledge. Share with the student what you notice about what she is doing. Personal positive acknowledgments, without judgments, build a trust gradually. The learner might think it strange at first to hear unfamiliar "I notice" statements. But her perspective will gradually shift from "Man, my teacher is weird today," to "My teacher is really watching me today," to "My teacher cares about me." Our intention is to build trust and build a relationship.

Some researchers suggest that the effective ratio of teacher comments is five positive to one negative. This concept might apply in "I notice" practice, however, we want to familiarize ourselves with the phrase at this stage. Let's focus simply on making ourselves experts on "I notice." If there are too many people in a group, you can plan whom you might focus on each day. "I notice" statements encourage kids and make them feel that we care about them. Soon they will want us to notice them more. Yes, they will start to want to form a relationship with us!

Here's another tip for "I notice" statements that are based on negative observation. When you make negative "I notice" comments, describe in as much detail as you can in a short sentence without any judgments, and then ask the child if they agree. If the student agrees, she can figure out how to improve. Or she might ask for help. If the student disagrees with your observation, you can figure out what keeps her from success by listening to her point of view. For instance, "Mary, I noticed your running speed is not as fast as last time. Did you notice? What do you think you can do differently next time?" Mary might say, "I will move my arms faster." Even if you don't agree with her idea, let her try her own solution. Let her fail! If Mary is a motivated child, she will come to you. "It doesn't work. What should I do, coach?" If Mary is hesitant (afraid!) to ask, you can approach her. "Would you like some suggestions? I suggest that you move your legs higher." (Notice the coach starting with "I.")

You might feel awkward using "I notice" statements at first, but pretty soon you will notice a different attitude from the children. Continue using "I notice" statements for a week. At the end of the week, write your self-reflection in a journal, starting with "I notice." For instance, "I notice I feel more comfortable using 'I notice' statements. I notice Mary is more eager to improve. I notice I feel happy when my gymnasts work hard." ANYTHING counts!

How "I Notice" Statements Work in My Classroom

Take one minute and think about your "I notice" practice. Here are some of my "I notice" statements to my students and their responses:

- I notice you look happy… "I am going to my brother's baseball game, so I am happy!"
- I notice you look tired… "I woke up in the middle of the night."
- I notice you are working on your morning task… (smile!)
- I notice your cool leggings… "I coordinated the color green!"
- I notice your legs are sticking outside of the desk legs… "Oops."

- I notice something on the floor... (Picks up a couple of pencils.)
- I notice you are struggling... "I know. Can I use the fraction kit?"

And then, I noticed someone who entered the classroom mad.

Me: I notice you are angry.

Kid: I AM very angry because Tom is annoying.

Me: Hmmm... (She just came in and is not interacting with Tom.)

Me: Hey, shall we step out? I will be glad to listen to you.

Kid: Fine. (Fuming!) (Follows me.)

Me: So, what's up?

Kid: Tom is making noises and it is so annoying.

Me: I see. You are frustrated because of the noise Tom makes, am I right?

Kid: Yes!

Me: Okay, why don't you let me talk to Tom? I assume you know some calming down strategies, am I right?

Kid: Right.

Me: Great. Let me go to talk to Tom and you take time to calm yourself down here. When you are settled, come back to the room.

Me: (Goes into the room.)

Kid: (Starts breathing.)

In a couple of minutes, she returned to the classroom and started her entry task. The whole conversation with her took five minutes. "I notice" statements gave her the impression "I care about you." This simple five-minute interaction saved many hours of instructional time. Adults who take care of children almost always have good intentions. Unfortunately, some people don't know how to communicate clearly. In these instances, people convey their good intention to their students by listening well instead of "telling" them how they care about them.

Building relationships starts with "I notice" statements. This also applies to adults (more on that in Week 3)!

<Journal Entry> (See Appendix B)

Now it's your turn. Your journal can be simple. Before your daily entry, pause and think about "I notice" statements you have made for the day. Once you have visualized them, start writing all of them down. If you didn't use an "I notice" statement, but you thought about it in your mind, note that. If you didn't think about it at all, note that as well. Be honest. If you think of something now that you didn't notice at the time, jot it down and let your learner know with an "I notice" statement tomorrow. Do this journal entry each day and share with your partner who is also working this program with you.

Week 2: Transform from "You" Statement to Questioning

Do you remember when you worked really hard at something and you still couldn't make it? What did your coach (teacher, parents, or any adult figure) tell you? What is the most effective method that you can adopt to encourage and keep engaging young learners and athletes in their activities?

In fourth grade, I worked hard on math story problems that had something to do with bananas and oranges. (You can read about this in my memoir, *Gift of Gratitude: Lessons from the Classroom*.) My teacher told me, "**You** don't have to know it," after I asked her about the same math question for the third time.

In tenth grade, I prepared a Beethoven sonata for an upcoming piano lesson. I wanted to impress my teacher with what he told me last time regarding the composer's emotion. After my extra hard work, he said, "**You** are not showing Beethoven's intention through this phrase."

In my junior year of college, I began to take swimming lessons. I even read a swimming book to improve my movement. In the next lesson, my coach said, "**Your** arms are moving awkwardly."

Notice how these teachers used "YOU" in their comments. "You" statements often happen when teachers or coaches are frustrated. You can almost see their thoughts during this time: "I have taught you this so many times. Why don't you get it????!!!!" As hard as they try to teach, their learners don't perform as well as they wish. Teachers feel desperate because of their inability to control the situation.

Here is an example scenario:

This student doesn't perform the way teacher explained. The teacher tells him, "You are wrong." The student tries again and does the same thing. The teacher says, "Why don't you try?" The third time, the teacher says, "How many times have I told you the same thing?"

STOP!

This scenario can change if we alter our thinking a little bit. This teacher just noticed the student isn't performing the way she explained. Now she says, "I noticed you are not performing the way I have explained. Do you have trouble understanding the instruction, or are you struggling with the process? Need help?" The student thinks about it for a moment and reviews and clarifies what his teacher expects. In his self-evaluating process, he feels ownership over his performance because the teacher is not telling him what to do. He is reflecting on how to improve his performance. Good question techniques and simple checking in are effective tools for ensuring your student's engagement and for building and maintaining positive relationships. The student also appreciates his coach paying attention to him and for sharing his observation.

Sometimes we aren't sure about whether or not a student is using their full potential when we notice that something is not working out as we expected. If a student is working his hardest, he may just need some quick guidance or to make a small adjustment. Consider the following example. Samuel was struggling with drawing straight lines with a ruler. Despite his hard work, his lines were not as straight as he expected. When I visited him, he complained, "Why can't I do it?" I asked him if I could see how he used his ruler. "I notice your pencil is UNDER the ruler," I said. Samuel replied, "What do you mean UNDER...? Oh, okay, I put my pencil right there..." He drew a straight line when he put a pencil against the top part of the ruler. I never said what to do, but he figured out how to succeed from the advice that he received.

If a student is not working with his full potential, there may be a variety of reasons behind his struggling. He might not feel well, something might be bothering him, etc. Mindful teachers will understand and will try to find out what the problem is so that they can adjust their advice. What if we approach with thoughtful words: "Do you feel okay?" "Do you have pain?" "Why don't you take a quick break?" The student will appreciate our compassion. We are making our students want to work for us.

Yes, when a student doesn't perform well, the teacher gets frustrated. However, a teacher's frustration won't fix a student's poor performance. Blaming a student's attitude and/or inability to conduct a project won't fix the problem. Additionally, blaming limits the student's potential. Only clear and compassionate communication will lead to success.

It is unfortunate when teachers blame learners for their own frustration. When teachers blame students with "You" comments, **teachers are only creating distance between them and their learners**.

Also, "You" statements are the "fixed" mindset language that creates fixed mindset learners. Labeling young learners sets limitations on them. When teachers label learners, they stop working hard because they think they have reached their limit. Learners begin to think that no matter how hard they work, their efforts won't be good enough.

This week, I propose to use questioning that will help learners become resilient.

What if my fourth grade teacher had asked me, "Can you tell me what you know so far?" Then, she might have continued with, "Well, this is what I think you are stuck on. What do you think?" Would I have tried again instead of giving up?

What if my piano teacher had asked me, "What do you think you did well in this piece? How do you know?" Then, he could have said, "I interpreted that part differently. Would you like to try it this way?" Would I have thought that there might be different ways to make certain expressions?

What if my swimming coach had asked me, "How did you use your arms today?" Then, she could have said, "I have some tips. Would you like to hear them?" Would I have been curious about another "trick" not in my book?

Questioning gives learners ownership of their own mistakes. They are the ones who are making mistakes. And they are the ones who are finding solutions—at least they think they are. Ownership empowers young learners, making them resilient. They come to want to make more mistakes because they believe mistakes make them grow.

Also, questioning creates a two-way relationship. Although the teachers' authority is highly respected, learners pay more attention to their own actions by answering the teachers' questions. In other words, they become more accountable for their performance.

Teachers/coaches must be the great navigators and facilitators who make their learners believe in themselves with Building Relationship Languages. While you are encouraging learners to believe in themselves, they are also learning to believe in you. Skillful questioning enhances our intention in the relationship.

In school and in sports, spontaneous things often happen. But before you react, take a breath and make growth mindset comments. "Wow, you did it! What is your strategy for making this work?" "Yikes, did you notice what went wrong?" Learners who see their mistakes as learning opportunities tend to outperform over those who believe in fixed mindsets (Dweck 2014). Students' minds are influenced by their teachers' growth mindset language.

Now, which phrase will you choose to say when you see your learners make mistakes? "You have to work harder," or "What do you think you have to do next?"

\<Journal Entry\> (See Appendix C)

List "I notice" statements for each day just as you have done in Week 1 and add questions that you used after your "I notice" statement. Have you noticed your consistency? Journaling is not too hard. But it does require a little bit of commitment, like one minute to reflect and five minutes of transcribing your memory. Meet up with your partner in person, on the phone, or over Skype. Share your success and celebrate!

As we are building on this great work habit, we are about to start Week 3! We will be talking about the relationship within ourselves. Let's move on!

Chapter 3

———

Connect to Ourselves

Week 3: I Notice Relationship within Ourselves

How did your Week 1 "I notice" task and Week 2 "Questioning" go? Did you come up with creative questions? Did you notice any differences, no matter how small? If you don't notice any differences yet, it's totally okay! It might take a while, but you will become more natural and confident with using the "I notice" phrase as you practice every day. Now, let's move onto this week's topic, "Build a Relationship with Yourself."

Think about when you raised your voice or you were sarcastic. Yelling reflects your frustration. Raising your voice is the result of anger. These extreme emotions make you react without thinking because of a part of our brain called amygdala, as previously discussed. In ancient times, primitive human beings survived life-threatening events thanks to the amygdala. Compared to our ancestors' lives, we have far less life-threatening events to face. As a result, small stimuli that are obviously non-life-threatening (like a student's poor performance) activate the amygdala. When you are calm, you understand this. You are not really angry at the child, but frustrated that the child's performance doesn't reflect your expectations. Your reaction is due to the situation that you cannot control.

While we explore different approaches for helping kids master their skills, we must remind ourselves that children's learning styles and paces vary. When nothing works for a student, stop struggling for one second and pause. Notice your feelings. If you notice that you're angry, you must take a deep breath. You are unlikely to use your "yelling" voice when you are calm. It is very important that you have the skill to NOTICE yourself (your emotion) during busy activity times. The good news is that you can train yourself to tune in.

What do I mean by a relationship with yourself? A common mistake that we often commit is making an assumption based on our hope. We believe that as long as we have a good intention, our message will be properly conveyed to our audience. Young learners must listen to teachers anyways, right? I have seen this proven wrong hundreds of times throughout my career as an educator. Without a positive relationship, we cannot assume that our listeners will accurately comprehend what we say. It doesn't matter how many times we say the same thing, our students' desire to learn through well-established relationships matters. When they don't comprehend what we say, how can they perform as we expect?

Let's suppose that I ask a student to open her notebook. "Are you ready to open to page 23?" She ignores me. I say, "Did you hear me? I said page 23." She keeps ignoring me. I become frustrated and raise my voice, which also sounds meaner in tone. "Excuse me, I am asking you to open the page." By this time, I am angry and in a rage. I am also embarrassed by my inability to control this child. Although following directions is a student's responsibility, my voice level and expression don't encourage her to want to change her behavior. Instead, this episode escalates until it is out of control. As a result, I become angrier. But did I notice I was angry?

I learned that I can break this vicious cycle by noticing my bodily sensations and emotions. When we experience anger, we are more likely to make dumb decisions. Afterwards, you might even feel remorseful or unable to follow through with promises that you made because the "fear, fight, and flight" part of the brain (amygdala) suppressed the logical part of the brain (prefrontal cortex). So how do we activate our prefrontal cortex to prevent this from happening? The only way we can diminish this heated feeling is, first, to notice it. As soon as we become aware of our strong emotion, we can tame it. Our awareness activates the prefrontal cortex, allowing us to make wiser decisions, such as using quieter voices and showing empathy or sadness.

Being angry is an emotion that anyone can experience. If you practice noticing when this strong emotion arises, you can pause and breathe. Breathing is a tool you can use to calm down. Breathe in fresh air and breathe out to relax your body. When you are calm, you can communicate better. Perhaps, you can whisper into that student's ear, "Hmmm, I would love to see page 23 when I come back." Don't let your emotions take over. Both noticing and embracing your feelings are essential for building a relationship with yourself.

Take Time to Engage with Ourselves

As you might have already noticed, it takes time to build a meaningful relationship with anyone, including yourself. A significant part of this week's challenge is to **start** and be **consistent**. When you start taking the time to practice noticing yourself during quiet moments, gradually you will also start noticing simple things (like your emotions, thoughts, and bodily sensations) during your busy daily routines. This is one example of mindfulness practice. This type of practice activates your prefrontal cortex, the part of the brain that controls logical thinking. This exercise fires neurons, re-wiring bad habits into new productive habits. Thus, this mindfulness practice will become your life-long treasure.

Through this simple practice, you can discover your inner self that you haven't noticed before.

This week, we are going to practice noticing what we feel and experience during a few minutes of quiet time every day. During this practice, focus on just one thing, like drawing your breath in and out. When you are distracted by thoughts, label them as "thoughts" and focus back on your breathing. This simple mindfulness exercise helps you to remain calm and to focus. Mindfulness apps, like Smiling Mind, offer guided practice if you wish for guidance. In fact, every morning, my students and I practice using Smiling Mind as part of our routine (read more details on this in my book, *Gift of Gratitude: Lessons from the Classroom*).

One day at a time, practice mindfulness meditation by noticing different things like sounds, physical sensations, emotions, and body parts, from your toes to your head. In each practice, use an "I notice" statement. For instance, "I notice my heart beating," "I notice someone talking outside of the room," "I notice my belly goes up and down," or "I notice I am fidgety." Let's jump into building a relationship with yourself!

Day 1: Two Minutes... Notice Your Breaths

Find a quiet spot where you can be alone. Sit on a chair. If your household is constantly busy, lock yourself in the bathroom and sit on the toilet! Then, set a timer for two minutes. The Online Meditation Timer will give you a peaceful gong sound at the end of the practice. During your very first two-minute session, focus on your nostrils, the air going in and out. You might also use your belly to feel your breath. The belly rises up and goes down. You can also count each breath, such as, "one, breathe in, two, breathe out, three, breathe in, four, breathe out." Notice each breath. When thoughts appear, label them "thoughts," and focus back on your belly. Don't judge, but notice.

<Journal Entry> (See Appendix D)

What did you notice among your learners today?

What questions did you ask today?

What did you notice during the two-minute mindful meditation?

Day 2: Three Minutes... Notice Your Breaths and Feelings

Set aside time for three minutes today. Use the same strategy from Day 1. Count each breath. Notice your breath. Notice your thoughts that come and go. Notice your feelings. "I notice my belly rises," "I notice my belly is empty," "I notice a thought came," "I feel fidgety," or "I feel peaceful," etc. Staying still for three minutes might be hard, but it is not impossible. If you succeed in keeping your eyes closed until the bell rings, give yourself a pat your shoulder.

<Journal Entry> (See Appendix D)

What did you notice during your meditation?

What did you notice among your learners?

What questions did you ask today?

Day 3: Five Minutes... Body Scan with a Flashlight

Today is a little more challenging. Find a quiet spot for five minutes. Pretend you are inside of your body, holding a flashlight. You are to light each part of your body from your toes, shins, knees, legs, hips, back, shoulders, arms, elbows, fingers, neck, ears, cheeks, chin, mouth, nose, and forehead. Then do the same thing in reverse. When thoughts distract you, focus back on your body. "I notice my toes," "I notice my shin," etc.

<Journal Entry> (See Appendix D)

What body parts did you light with your flashlight clearly?

What did you notice among your learners today?

What questions did you ask today?

Day 4: Five Minutes... Body Scan and Body Sensations

You guessed it! Find your (regular!) quiet spot and set a timer for five minutes. Just like you did yesterday, mentally light each part of your body from the bottom to the top. Today, notice not only each body part, but also notice sensations. "I notice my fingers are tingly," "I notice my heart is beating," "My head is warm," etc.

<Journal Entry> (See Appendix D)

What sensations did you experience?

What did you notice among your learners today?

What questions did you ask today?

Day 5: Five Minutes... Body Scan, Body Sensations, and Emotions

Keep your routine as much as you can. Same spot and same time. Remember to continue mindfulness meditation practice throughout this program and throughout your life, because building relationships takes time. Particularly today, notice your emotions while you scan your body. Do you feel agitated, uncomfortable, peaceful, frustrated, calm, or anything else? Do you experience different feelings during five short minutes? When you are done, pause and notice your emotions.

<Journal Entry> (See Appendix D)

What body parts did you notice clearly?

What sensations did you feel?

What feelings do you experience during meditation?

What did you notice among your learners today?

What questions did you ask today?

Day 6: Five Minutes... Mindful Listening

Set your timer for five minutes. Today, you will focus on the sounds around you, near and far. What noise did you notice nearest to you or farthest? When you get distracted, bring your focus back to the sounds.

<Journal Entry> (See Appendix D)

What sound did you hear nearest to you?

What sound did you hear farthest from you?

What did you notice among your learners today?

What questions did you ask today?

Day 7: Mindful Eating

No timer required. Bring a piece of chocolate or a fruit. First, put it on your palm and look at it. Then, bring it up to your ear and listen to it. Next, bring it to your nose and smell it. Finally, put it on your tongue—but don't chew yet. Observe the food's texture and taste in your mouth. Which part of your tongue tastes it? Now chew carefully.

What flavor do you taste? Is there more than one flavor? Now swallow. How far can you follow the food traveling inside of your body?

<Journal Entry> (See Appendix D)

Jot down everything that you noticed during this observation, such as looks, smells, sounds, feels, and tastes. Describe in as much detail as possible.

What did you notice among your learners today? (If you had contact time with learners.)

What questions did you ask today? (If you had contact time with learners.)

What We Expect From Our Experiences

How do you feel? Strange? Awkward? Have you experienced a kind of peacefulness? If you notice that there is no change, let's celebrate, because "no change" is what you are experiencing right at this moment. Simply continue to notice yourself during these five minutes of silence every day. Each practice activates neurons that fire and re-wire. Your brain is creating a space where you can pause!

Building relationships with your young learners starts from you. As you experience calmness, you bring it into the relationship with others. When you experience anger, notice it and step back until calmness returns. You can revisit the issue or person later when you are calm. Even if you think you might waste the learning momentum by pausing, you are actually saving a lot of time because you will certainly be able to communicate with your students better when you are calm. Students will understand your intention and the message that you want to convey at a deeper level.

You have just learned how to connect to yourself. Continue setting aside the same time and place for this week's practice in the following weeks. Soon, you will be able to apply visualization and self-affirmation during your mindfulness meditation practice. We will talk more about that in Week 5.

Chapter 4

Extend "I Notice" Statement

Week 4: I Notice Colleagues, Family Members, and Other Adults

Congratulations! We have been practicing "I notice" statements with our learners and ourselves for the past three weeks! Keep up with it, and also continue with your daily five-minute noticing practice that we started last week.

This week, we will extend relationship building to the wider community in addition to ourselves and our students because we are becoming an expert of the "I notice" statement! Yes, our colleagues and family members are people with whom we want to practice making better connections with, even if our connections are already positive. Intentional acknowledgement and kindness cheer people up at any age. This is a great opportunity to demonstrate in front of students how adults should treat each other. How important is that?

48

Start Simple

Simply speaking, when someone (an acquaintance or maybe even a stranger!) approaches us with smile, we're likely to feel at ease and relaxed. We can be open. If we add a compliment to someone with "I notice," these simple words will brighten up their day. Some examples include "I noticed your new shoes" (to a co-worker), "I noticed you have done laundry" (to a spouse), or "I noticed you lowered your body when you were talking to your student" (to a new teacher). "I notice your positive energy this morning" (to a co-worker), "I notice parents are happy with your work" (to an employee), and "I feel fortunate to work with you" (to a supervisor). Even smiling at your staff makes a huge difference in the community.

"I notice" opportunities are limitless! Soon, we will begin noticing how our working communities, neighborhoods, and our families change each day. In the meantime, we will notice our own feelings more and more frequently, especially, when we get responses for our "I notice" statements. Some of you might still wonder, "Why do I have to deal with my colleagues, families, and communities? I just want to build a relationship with kids!" Here is why.

Positive Outcomes from Modeling

Kids are watching you, directly and indirectly. Whether we are talking directly to our students or to someone else (adults), students sense several relationships in the learning community. Students gradually look up to your friendly and respectful communication style. We want to hang out with someone who is nice to others, regardless of age. Intentional communications among adults inspire students. As a result, they desire to connect with you. Adults' positive interactions and relationships will impact students' attitudes and their performance. So we have to start within ourselves, instead of waiting for someone to come to us.

If you are an overachiever, extend the "I notice" compliment exercise to your family members. "I notice you have watered the plants!" "I notice you used a new spice on the dish," "I notice you got a haircut," etc. Each of our comments makes our relationships tighter! These comments are what we are going to keep in our journal for this week.

<Journal Entry> (See Appendix E)

You are getting better at noticing each day. When you feel a strong emotion during the day, notice it and just breathe. Emotion is like a floating cloud. Though some emotions might disturb you, they will eventually go away. Be kind to yourself; allow whatever emotion it is to come in, and breathe. Now you can gently let go. Notice that you are calmer as you speak to your learners.

You can answer each question as a guide in the journal worksheet (Appendix E). Reflection represents a significant part of relationship building. When your experience and emotion are integrated in the daily journal, your learning memories become accessible in your brain. It means you are creating a good habit during the process of building a relationship.

Within Ourselves

How do you feel when you are intentionally building a relationship?

What bodily sensations do you feel?

What feelings do you experience during meditation?

With Learners

What did you notice among your learners today?

What questions did you ask today?

With Colleagues

What did you notice among your colleagues today?

We are now halfway through! Your commitment is remarkable! Look at your partner and exchange high-fives! Next week, we will introduce "I notice" statements to our learners and encourage them to use them throughout the day.

Week 5: Introduce and Practice "I Notice" with Children

We are now ready to share what we have learned so far with our learners. The first day of this week, we are going to have a mini-meeting about "I notice" statements. As we have experienced, noticing something takes extra effort. But think about it this way, each time we make the effort to notice something, our brain fires and re-wires.

When we use "I notice" statements to build better relationships with our students, simultaneously, we develop better focus within ourselves. When our students focus and are able to notice their own performance, they are going to develop a genuine desire to learn from you. This is when learners are truly receptive to our advice. Yes, "I notice" statements bring us intentional focus and compassionate relationships.

How Self-Awareness Impacts Students' Learning

When learners become aware of what's happening around themselves in the moment—noticing something as simple as their breathing, body movement, bodily sensations, or emotions—their focusing skills improve. While students practice to notice their internal and external experiences, their nervous system shifts to the right gear (Siegel 2014) to focus. Gradually, self-awareness is developed and it becomes powerful and effective in a more complicated learning process. When students take the initiative to analyze their own performance and search for solutions, their performance becomes more sophisticated.

However, as we might have already experienced, noticing things is not easy. The simplest things can prove very challenging. Thus, it is quite normal for kids to feel that it's too difficult to remain still and quiet for one full minute.

With Guided Meditation App

This is where a guided meditation app, such as Smiling Mind, comes to the rescue. I have been using Smiling Mind in my classroom for three years. Listening to the appropriate guide is helpful for all students—even fidgety ones. The students' responses are overwhelmingly positive. Practicing daily "I notice" exercises not only empowers individual students, but it also creates connectedness among students in the learning community.

With Teacher's Familiar Voice

Using the teacher's own voice is the most effective option during an "I notice" session with students. Since our students are used to our tone of voice, they perceive our positive intentions naturally. Also, this practice creates a mindful sense of community. Students can connect to each other by sharing their moments together. Now, set a timer for one minute, just like when we practiced.

How Mindfulness Meditation Works in My Classroom

Here is an example of what I say to my students before a one-minute mindful meditation.

"Champions (I love calling my learners champions!), I have something I would love to share today. You may or may not have noticed, but I have been using 'I notice' statements for a while. This has been great for me because when I teach (coach or train) you, I can focus better on your performance.

"I have learned that 'noticing' is a powerful focusing tool for both teachers and learners.

"This week, we are going to practice one-minute mindfulness practices. Mindfulness exercises help us focus better. We are going to sit on the floor with our legs crossed, close our eyes, and breathe slowly. Imagine you are inside of your body, lighting a flashlight at each part of your body. And notice how you feel. Notice your body's sensations. At the end of one minute, tell me what you noticed."

Day 1: Count Your Breaths

"Please be ready for your mindfulness body. (Straight back, eyes closed, legs crossed or sitting on the chair.)

"Find your anchor. (Hands on their belly, chest, or under the nose.)

"Breathe in, breathe out.

"Count each breath.

"One, breathe in, two, breathe out, up to ten. Then start over."

Bell rings (timer).

"How do you feel? Are you focused? Let's start today!"

At the end of the practice, ask your students, "What did you notice about your practice?" If you have already established the individual reflection routine, encourage your students to use the "I notice" statement, instead of "My accomplishment is…" or "I did…" These "I notice" statements encourage ownership of their accomplishments.

<Journal Entry> (See Appendix F)

We will include some of our students' "I notice" comments. Which "I notice" comments made by your students surprised you? Let's continue our own "I notice" exercise. Remember to meet up and share your observations with your partner this week.

Day 2: Scan Your Body

"Mindfulness Body. (Sit up straight.)

"Anchor. (Hands on their belly, chest, or under the nose.)

"Breathe in, breathe out.

"Today, you are going to explore inside your body with a flashlight. As I mention a body part, light that part with your flashlight. Let's begin.

"Find your toes and light them. Ankles. Now your shins. Knees. Legs. Hips.

"Belly. Back. Shoulders. Elbows. Wrists. Fingers. Chest. Neck.

"Face. Ears. Forehead. And eyes.

"Take a big breath in, (pause) and let it out.

"When you no longer hear the bell, you can open your eyes."

Bell rings (timer). Smile when you meet your students' eyes.

\<Note\>

Remember to reinforce "I notice" statements throughout the day and encourage a reflective conversation at the end. Keep your learners' "I notice" comments as well as your own in your journal.

Day 3: Listen to Your Surroundings

"Mindfulness body.

"Anchor. (Hands on belly, chest, or under the nose.)

"Breathe in, breathe out."

"Today, we will focus on the sounds around us. After the bell, we will share the closest sound you hear and the furthest sound you hear." (Set the timer for one minute.)

<Debrief with Students>

"What was the closest sound?

"What was the furthest sound?

"You can practice this at home so that you can improve your focusing skills. Great job!

"Let's begin our day!"

Day 4: Visualize Yourself

"Mindfulness body. (Sit with straight back.)

"Find your anchor. (Hands on your belly, chest, or under the nose.)

"Breathe in, breathe out."

Set the timer for one minute and say:

"You are going to visualize yourself today. What skill (handwriting, spelling test, math story problem, shooting a hoop, balancing on the beam) do you want to work on today? Imagine you are doing this skill step by step in your head.

"Which body part might help you succeed with your skill?

"Visualize yourself performing this skill well.

"How do you feel when you accomplish this skill in your vision?" Timer ends.

\<Debrief with Students\>

"What bodily sensations did you notice when you visualized your accomplishment?"

Day 5: Send Gratitude

"Mindfulness body. (Sit up straight.)

"Anchor. (Hands on their belly, chest, or under their nose.)

"Breathe in, breathe out."

Set the timer for one minute and say:

"Think about one person who cares about you, supports your activities, and helps your dreams come true.

"Put your hands over your heart.

"Visualize that person very clearly. And tell that person how grateful you feel for him/her."

<Optional>

"You are going to write whom you sent your gratitude today. How do you feel? Now, open your eyes and let's begin to write in your journal."

To get your FREE Gratitude Journal Template, email me with the topic "gratitude journal" at claire.e.hallinan@gmail.com.

<Debrief>

"How do you feel when you are sending your gratitude?"

Chapter 5

———

Strengthen Learners' Mindset through Daily Routine Communication Pathway

Over the last five weeks, we have learned how to connect to ourselves, to our learners, and to other people in our learning community. We are going to visualize what has been happening in our lives. Let's dive into this by drawing and coloring. For this exercise, we will need a journal, a pencil, and some colored pencils.

Let's go find the blank space at Appendix G and draw a dot in the middle of a blank box. That represents you. You used to be this single dot, but when you started connecting yourself by using "I notice" statements, this dot became a circle. Draw a circle around the dot. Pick your favorite color, and color inside of the circle.

Now draw another dot and connect your circle to this dot with a line. This line is the connection you had with your student. As you connect to your student through exercise, one line becomes two lines. The student's dot changes into a circle and you become a double circle. Color each space (within the circles and the connecting lines) with your favorite colors. With each practice, you build a wider pathway as well as space in yourself.

A wide pathway filters the same amount of water faster than a narrow one. In this instance, water refers to the level of acceptance in communication. The wider the pathway, the more water goes through. This means that the maximum amount of information that a teacher provides is delivered clearly through the widened pathway. So the student absorbs with ease. The student can also reach out to their teacher through this communication pathway. This clear and wide pathway is smooth and nothing really gets stuck between teacher and students.

As we practiced each weekly task, the teacher and the student's circle increased in size and became more colorful. The sizes and colors of the circles represent the space that you created through "I notice" practice. This practice helped us to accept our emotions, to focus on our tasks, and to choose the best words to communicate with our students. Consistent practice made our circle larger and more colorful. Consistent practice made our student's circle larger and more colorful. And consistent practice made the communication stronger and variegated. However, we cannot stop our practices quite yet.

Consistency is a key factor in building intentional communication. If you want to play a beautiful piece on the piano, you must practice every day. If you want to win a gold medal on the track, you must practice every day. If you want to keep space in your brain, you must practice every day.

Let's look at the page we have created. This is how we have built intentional relationships with our students. When a relationship is established intentionally, our students are ready to absorb our message at the maximum capacity with minimum effort, just like water flowing through the wide pathway. How colorful, how large each circle, how wide each connection—these are all essential components of strong relationships.

How do you feel now? How wide is your pathway with your students? What size is your circle? How about your student's circle? Believe it or not, every daily practice that you have done has contributed to building and strengthening a meaningful relationship. How do you sustain it? The answer is consistency. Don't underestimate the pathway. It can rust and break if you don't work hard every day.

How challenging was it before we had established an "intentional" relationship? We have been working on creating sustainable relationships by connecting to ourselves and to others. If you are working with your partner, share your graphics. Share memorable episodes. You are integrating each practice with your observations and emotions so that your experiences become more meaningful, vivid memories in the hippocampus. Boy, you have come a long way.

Now sit back and think again about why relationships are important. Why should relationships be intentional? A great relationship motivates your learners to perform better. We (all educators) want our learners to succeed, out-perform, and exceed our expectations. We are building relationships with our students by observing (not criticizing) ourselves, our students, and all other learning community members. This "noticing" skill helps us connect to and understand our students; it also helps our students connect to and understand themselves and each other.

This week, we are going to explore how to sustain this good habit that we have established. We don't have to be perfect, but we can continue to make the communication/trust pathway stronger and wider.

Let's keep up with "I notice" statements in our journal. We are already familiar with "I notice" statements. Meet up with your partner once a week to celebrate. Students have been noticing our change, willingness, and care in the relationship. We are creating a good habit by being consistent. Students are now ready to listen to you and desire to receive your expertise! It is time to establish sustainable routines and celebrations.

Week 6 and Beyond

Let's continue with our previous routines every day. They are working! We have accumulated many accomplishments from Week 1 through Week 5 and we need to sustain them. If we need a reminder, make a note and stick it on the desk or our planner.

Through a Wider Pathway

In the beginning of our journey, we noticed that our students don't necessarily digest our messages as much as we want. "You" statements, in particular, block our relationship pipe. As you may recall, this is why we practiced "I notice" statements. How do our relationships with students, and with ourselves, improve? Let's visualize.

Consider the picture you have drawn. You and your student are no longer dots. Teacher and students are now both large, colorful circles. Our students are ready to learn everything that we are going to teach through our well-established pathway. And we also have more space in ourselves to respond to our students.

Instead of giving our students step-by-step instructions on what to do and how to do it, why don't we teach them how to figure out challenges by themselves? We can teach our students how to visualize success and believe in their effort. Teachers can guide and facilitate students during their learning process. What we want to teach students this week is the growth mindset.

Growth Mindset through the Wide Communication Pathway

Mindset is such an important factor when it comes to learning. Regardless of subjects, topics, or skills, having a proper mindset makes your students strong learners. Strong learners obtain 1) ownership of their own learning, 2) desire to achieve, and 3) belief in hard work. We often underestimate the power of the mind, but having the right mindset makes learners engage with their activities and desire to succeed.

A person with a fixed mindset believes that they have a certain amount of talent and abilities and that's that. On the other hand, a person with a growth mindset sees talents and abilities as things they can develop (Dweck 2009).

This week and beyond, we will implement growth mindset feedback—this is especially important when students are mentally blocked. For instance, students might say, "I can't do this," "You are asking me too much," "It's too hard," or "I am not as good as Stephen." Our feedback should not start with "You." As described in the earlier chapter, "You" statements block the relationship pathway. When a student says, "I can't do this," you often reply, "Yes, you can." "I can't do this" is a product of the student's frustration. Our task is to navigate this frustration into hopeful waters by adding one simple word: "yet." By simply adding "yet," the statement transforms from desperation to determination, inspiring the student to continue to work hard. "I can't do this, yet." How powerful is that?

The best part is that the student will explore different approaches in order to succeed. We can offer, "Would you like to have some suggestions?" (Cline, Fey 2014). When you have a wide pathway, your students desire to hear your suggestions!

Here is a list of Feedback Language examples with a growth mindset. We are going to use one at a time. Choose one statement before class begins and write it down on a sticky note. This means that your feedback today is intentional. You want your students to focus on effort, not results. If possible, practice these examples a few times in advance. Then wait for the moment when you can use them.

Examples of Feedback Language with Growth Mindsets:

- Look at how much progress you made on this!
- Let's stop here and return in a few minutes with a fresher brain.
- We can always fix mistakes once I see where you are getting help.
- I want you to remember for a moment how challenging this was when you began.
- The next time you have a challenge like this, what will you do?

Notice how differently your students respond to your intentional feedback with a growth mindset compared to previous feedback. Jot down on sticky notes how you feel during conversations with your students. That is going to be our treasure forever. Put the date on it and stick it in your journal. When you see your partner this week, share your detailed experiences with each other. Remember, neurons in your brain fire and re-wire when experiences integrate with your stories and emotions (Siegel, Payne 2014). And your brain stores these integrated memories. Our brains have been wired in a negative pattern. Once a habit is made, we tend to stay in the same pattern. The only way we can create a healthy pattern is to try new and different things. Neurons will fire and **re-wire** and create new paths, patterns, and habits in the brain.

Establish Rituals/Routine and Celebrate!

Building an intentional relationship is simple, yet it requires flexibility in our thinking patterns. Once we establish "I notice" statements, we experience some benefits, such as space to pause within ourselves when we are upset. We no longer yell at students! Another benefit is the formation of a wider communication pathway. Through the wide communication pathway, our good intention is well-received among students. We can sustain this pathway with our daily effort.

When we have the ability to pause and breathe, we can connect pathways to several different students. At the same time, students can also connect to each other; they can learn from each other. This is the ideal learning community that both students and teachers appreciate being in. Let's establish some routines for intentional positive relationships in the learning community.

1. Before Students Enter the Classroom

Stand at the door where students enter. Relationships start here. Greet each student individually and share something you notice, such as "Good morning, I notice you have a new haircut today." By verbalizing our observations, they will cement as memories in our brain. We can incorporate some of these observations into lessons, such as writing prompts and math problems. Be creative. When we use our observation of a certain student, we are building stronger connections with him. This is a win-win routine.

2. Morning Meeting

Gather all students into a circle and guide them in a one-minute mindfulness practice session. (Continue for up to five minutes, if desired. Reference Week 5.) Facilitate their sharing of how they feel today and, if necessary, why they feel this way.

3. Throughout the Day

Pause when we notice ourselves agitated because the class is noisy or some students don't get along, etc. This pause gives us a better communication language, tone of voice, and calmness. "Hmmm, I notice that our voice level is a little too high. What shall we do to make our voice a level 1?" "I notice you are stuck on this problem. What tool might help on your problem?"

In the beginning of activities or transition, visualization helps learners regulate themselves. "Visualize working with your partner. What words are you using? How are you working with her?" Students listen to us because our voices are naturally going through the wide pathway you have established.

4. Growth Mindset Poster

Quite a few growth mindset posters are available on Pinterest. Choose one of your favorites, post it on the classroom wall, and refer to it as needed. We talk about each line during the morning meeting. Through the wide pathway, teachers need to send messages about the importance of hard work, taking risks, making mistakes, and wanting to learn. By doing this, teachers will discourage students from relying on just their talents.

5. Communication with Families

Parents always want to know how their child is doing in the classroom. Once a week, send a quick group email discussing what you've noticed. It can be simple. Celebrate some students' accomplishments during the week, and make sure you cover all individual students at least every other month. As families are happy to receive our observations (what we noticed about their child), we can make the family communication pathway wider. When the communication pathway is wider, it will be easier to bring up difficult subjects as they arise. This is because the families understand your positive intention through the relationships you have established.

6. Closing Meeting

The closing meeting is as important as the morning meeting. In my class, students enter three items in their gratitude journal and share what they are grateful for each day. Peer recognition (the classmate's name and the actions they took) is a powerful tool for promoting appreciation. As a result, students can build intentional relationships among themselves. Another option could be a celebration of what they noticed during the day. Acknowledgment and celebration transform an individual from a dot to a bigger and more colorful circle. The student's appreciation for the comments widens the communication pathway.

7. At the Final Bell

Give a high-five to each student as a final celebration for the day! Give as short a comment as possible, such as, "It was a fun discussion in the reading group, wasn't it?" "Are you ready for the next math challenge?" "I look forward to seeing your homework again tomorrow morning!" Make as many smiles as possible!

\<Journal Entry\> (See Appendix I)

1. Which routine would like to adopt in your schedule? How?

2. Do you need any support for this new routine?

3. How do you feel?

Chapter 6

Reflection

Congratulations! You have reached the final chapter. During the last six weeks, we have gained skills for building relationships. These are the skills we have developed:

1. Communicating with observation ("I notice") statements, not judgmental "You" statements.

2. Connecting within yourself by engaging in a five-minute mindful practice session every day.

3. Creating a mindful community by leading a one-minute (up to five minutes) mindful practice with your students every day.

4. Encouraging learners with growth mindsets.

Let's look back to your first entry in your journal. You listed some of your students whom you want to improve relationships with, why you want to improve those relationships, and what you want to accomplish from these relationships. Over the past few weeks, have you noticed any progress?

Remember my student Josh? He was lazy and didn't seem to listen to my suggestions. He wouldn't try anything by himself, even though I told him he has so much potential! I wanted him to pay attention when I talked. Your student might be similar or have different challenges. Now you are going to reflect on what you have done and how your view of the student has transformed.

After two years with Josh, I concluded that he was not lazy. When I first met him, he hadn't learned how to focus on the academic field yet. In fact, he could focus on his favorite cartoon characters and engage in a conversation about them forever! As I increased "I notice" statements, Josh gradually opened up and began searching for my suggestions on how to perform academic tasks. Also, he started to show remorse when he didn't bring his homework to class. One day, he announced, "I will stay in at recess to finish my homework." It didn't happen every day, but think about his growth—from nothing to something. Josh started to notice what he was missing and thought about what he must do. He took a missing assignment as an opportunity to learn instead of a fatal mistake. This is strong evidence of neurons firing to connect new pathways and re-wiring old, unproductive habits to productive ones over time. Each time the neuron sparks, the specific behavior pattern is strengthened. That is why we must continue practicing intentional relationships.

Now, let's discuss your ups and downs as well as your students'. Write each response in your journal and share it with your partner. (Appendix J)

1. What did you feel about yourself over the course?

2. Did you notice calmness in yourself? Pleasantness? When? How did it happen?

3. Have you experienced any frustration? How did you overcome it?

4. How has your student changed, or are they the same (attitude, skill improvement)?

5. How would you describe the relationship between you and the student?

Building intentional relationships truly transforms student potential. It all starts when you notice!

Bibliography

Cline, Foster, Fey, Jim (2014) *Parenting with Love and Logic: Teaching Children Responsibility, NavPress.*

Cozolino, Louis, (2014) *The Neuroscience of Human Relationships 2nd edition Attachment and the Developing Social Brain,* 2014, W.W. Norton 7 Company Inc.

Dweck, Carol, (2009) *Mindsets: Developing Talent Through a Growth Mindset,* Olympic Coach Volume 21 Number 1.

Fey, Jim, Funk, David (1995) *Teaching with Love and Logic Taking Control of the Classroom,* Love and Logic Press.

Hattie, John, *(2012) Visible Learning for Teachers: Maximizing Impact on Learning,* Routledge

Lehrer, Jonah, *The Mirror Neuron Revolution: Explaining What Makes Humans Social,* Mind Matters.

Siegel, Daniel J. M.D. and Payne, Bryson, Tina, Ph.D, (2011) *The Whole-Brain Child:*

12 Revolutionary Strategies to Nurture Your Child's Developing Mind, Survive Everyday Parenting Struggles, and Help Your Family Thrive, A Bantam Books Trade Paperback.

Winerman, Lea, (2005) The mind's mirror, American Psychological Association, Vol 36, No. 9.

Appendix A: Journal Worksheet

Pre-Evaluation

Date	Journal	Notes, Discussions, Questions, Resources
	1) List some of your learners with whom you want to improve your current relationship.	
	2) List why you want to improve your relationship	
	3) List what you hope this improved relationship will accomplish.	

Appendix B: Journal Worksheet Observation Not Judgment

Week 1: I Notice Statement in Relationship with Children

Date	What did I notice in the children today?	Notes, Discussions, Questions, Resources
	Day 1 • I notice • • • **Day 2** • I notice • • • **Day 3** • I notice • • • **Day 4** • I notice • • •	

Day 5
- I notice
-
-
-

Day 6
- I notice
-
-
-

Day 7
- I notice
-
-
-

Appendix C: Journal Worksheet Observation Not Judgment

Week 2: I Notice Statement in Relationship with Children + Questioning

Date	What did I notice in the children today?	What question did I ask today?
	Day 1 • I notice • •	**Day 1** • • •
	Day 2 • I notice • •	**Day 2** • • •
	Day 3 • I notice • •	**Day 3** • • •
	Day 4 • I notice • •	**Day 4** • • •
	Day 5 • I notice • •	**Day 5** • • •
	Day 6 • I notice • •	**Day 6** • • •
	Day 7 • I notice • •	**Day 7** • • •

Appendix D: Journal Worksheet Observation Not Judgment

Week 3: I Notice Statements in Relationship with Ourselves

Date	Journal
	Day 1 • What did you notice among your learners today? • What questions did you ask today? • What physical sensations and/or emotions did you notice during your two-minute mindful meditation? **Day 2** • What did you notice among your learners? • What questions did you ask today? • What feelings did you notice during your meditation? **Day 3** • What did you notice among your learners today? • What questions did you ask today? • What body parts did you light with your flashlight clearly? **Day 4** • What did you notice among your learners today? • What questions did you ask today? • What sensations did you experience?

Day 5

- What did you notice among your learners today?

- What questions did you ask today?

- What body parts did you notice clearly?

- What sensations did you feel?

- What feelings did you experience during meditation?

Day 6

- What did you notice among your learners today?

- What questions did you ask today?

- What sound did you hear nearest to you?

- What sound did you hear farthest from you?

Day 7

- Jot down everything that you noticed during this observation, such as looks, smells, sounds, feels, and taste. Describe in as much detail as possible.

- What did you notice among your learners today?

- What questions did you ask today?

Appendix E: Journal Worksheet Connect to Learning Community

Week 4: I Notice Statements in Relationship with Colleagues, Family Members, and Other Adults

Remember to date when you enter each topic for the week.

Date	Journal
	Within Ourselves • How do you feel when you are building a relationship intentionally? • What body sensation did you feel? • What feeling did you experience during meditation? **With Learners** • What did you notice among your learners today? • What questions did you ask today? **With Colleagues** • What did you notice among your colleagues today?

Appendix F: Journal Worksheet Connect to Learning Community

Week 5: Introduce and Practice "I Notice" with Children

Date	Journal	Notes, Discussions, Questions
	Day 1 • What did you notice among your learners today? • What feelings did you experience during your meditation? • What did you notice in students after Count Your Breath practice? • **Day 2** • What did you notice among your learners today? • What feelings did you experience during your meditation? • What did you notice in students after Scan Your Body practice? •	

Day 3

- What did you notice among your learners today?

- What feelings did you experience during your meditation?

- What did you notice in students after Listen to Your Surroundings practice?

-

Day 4

- What did you notice among your learners today?

- What feelings did you experience during your meditation?

- What did you notice in students after Visualize Yourself practice?

-

Day 5

- What did you notice among your learners today?

- What feelings did you experience during your meditation?

- What did you notice in students after Sending Gratitude practice?

-

Appendix G: Journal Worksheet

Strengthen Learners' Mindset through Daily Routine

Week 6 and Beyond: Visualize Your Success

Date	Journal	Notes, Discussions, Questions
	Day 1 • What did you notice among your learners today? • What feelings did you experience during your meditation? • What skills do you notice in your students? **Day 2** • What did you notice among your learners today? • What feelings did you experience during your meditation? • What skills do you notice in your students? **Day 3** • What did you notice among your learners today? • What feelings did you experience during your meditation? • What skills do you notice in your students?	

Day 4
- What did you notice among your learners today?

- What feelings did you experience during your meditation?

- What skills do you notice in your students?

Day 5
- What did you notice among your learners today?

- What feelings did you experience during your meditation?

- What skills do you notice in your students?

Appendix H: Journal Worksheet
Communication Pathway

Date:

Appendix I: Journal Worksheet Establish Rituals/Routine and Celebrate!

	Journal
	• Which routine would like to adopt in your schedule?
	• How?
	• Do you need any support for this new routine?
	• How do you feel?

Appendix J: Journal Worksheet Final Reflection

Date as you complete each question.

Date	Journal
	<ul><li>How did you feel about yourself over the course of the book?</li><li>Did you notice calmness in yourself? Pleasantness? When? How did it happen?</li><li>Have you experienced any frustration? How did you get over it?</li><li>How has this student changed (attitude, skill improvement)?</li><li>How would you describe the relationship between you and the student?</li></ul>

Made in the USA
Coppell, TX
27 July 2021